POETRY BY ANTONIA WANG

*Love Bites: Poetry & Prose*

*In the Posh Cocoon: Poetry and Bits of Life*

*Hindsight 2020: Brief Reflections on a Long Year*

*Retrospectiva 2020: Reflexiones Breves Sobre un Año Largo*

*Palette: Love Poems and Painted Words*

*Matices: Poemas de Amor y Paisajes del Alma*

*Things I Could Have Said in One Line But Didn't: Poems on Love,
Relationships and Existentialism*

# things I could have said

POEMS ON LOVE, RELATIONSHIPS AND EXISTENTIALISM

# but didn't

BY ANTONIA WANG

Written and published by Antonia Wang
Photo art by Antonia Wang
Edited by Ty Gardner

First paperback and ebook editions: February 2023

ISBN: 979-8-9860457-3-3 (ebook)
ISBN: 979-8-9860457-4-0 (paperback)

Manufactured in the United States of America

biteslove.com

Like missed baggage we sit
in places that have names
unknown to our claimants
who fret in other places
at speeds and pressures
that split all things apart
a condition necessary
perhaps   to the birthing of stars
but fatal   to simple pairing
necessary to recognition
and the claiming of our own.


~ Richard O. Moore
Writing the Silences

# Contents in One Line

| | |
|---|---|
| Truth lives in the silence, | 67 |
| with an almost pang of lust, | 68 |
| clueless that we orbit love, | 69 |
| I won't quench your thirst. | 70 |
| Then, they burst the heart. | 71 |
| stars swallowed me whole | 72 |
| If I forget you | 73 |
| ablaze with the first touch. | 74 |
| I read every word. | 75 |
| to feed while I sleep. | 76 |
| lush with longing— | 77 |
| she is now a beacon | 78 |
| for the rift inside my chest, | 79 |
| I was wrong. | 80 |
| landforms between us. | 81 |
| I live for you. | 82 |
| Words are pointless | 83 |
| and still I melt | 84 |
| you diffused my veins. | 85 |
| She seems different | 86 |
| I still smile for you, | 87 |
| There was no message | 88 |
| in love, all is fair | 89 |
| you explode with light | 90 |
| He is never coming back, | 91 |
| awaiting a spark of magic, | 92 |
| pixelated under my eyelids | 93 |

# Part I: But We Don't Talk About It

We can all write about suffering
with our eyes closed. You should show
people more of yourself; show them your
clandestine passion for red meat.

~ Louise Glück

*Metastasis*

He won't listen to me now, or ask why.
Now that I am waterproof,
he can drown me in his silence.

When he looks at me, I can tell
how long it's been since Sirius crashed
his irises at the thought of me.

Now that I have metastasized in his skin,
he doesn't need to touch me
but he knows when I move around

planting things. He can hear me eat.
Will I consume him? No doubt, but

we don't talk about it.

He won't ask why his body is an itch,
or why his pores keep sprouting
Black-eyed Susans.

*Forgotten Promises*

Don't wake me yet. I want to stay
in the green ebony forest we didn't hike.

I've been going back at night

through a tiny door in the closet.

A man I once knew runs the place.
He turns the waterfalls on
for me, and hands me a blanket
my grandma knit. He leaves me
alone with a talking fire.

We chat all night about Green Ebony,
how hard it is to burn its mossy bark.
Part of me laments
not moving here, as if I'd broken

a (forgotten) promise. I fall
asleep on a hollow log,
wake up in my bed.
Grandma sneaks into my bedroom
through a hole in my head.

She rubs it closed
with one of her balms.
She's sorry, she says, she couldn't
meet me in the forest,
or ever learned how to knit.

*Convenience*

One day she'll leave, play out every scene
in her shopworn daydreams:

a job in the city
that never sleeps, a nap with God
in a concrete hammock, a roof
in the mountains…

a pressed-linen husband
dressed in white,
and all the bedding
conformity can buy.

For now, she breathes.

Her legs waltz her
behind a counter where she sells
trinkets to the undead.

An eagle-winged friend swoops by,
and pities her.
It's good to see her, too.

She clocks out, her burlap arms
filled with groceries—
enough to feed a sponger lover
and two sawdust children.

*Scrapbooking*

Venus lit her eyes like tinder,
yet she longs
for things she can't touch.

Life is over now.

Time froze
in the murmur of a burning
wheat field.

No one grieves it
or remembers
why we made it law.

She pours boiling, crushed cacao
in her scrapbook of creature comforts,
to archive this dead-hearted day.

Carmine lips and cheeks,
coarse laughter masking the yawning
exhaustion of a world with no end.

Dogs howl at the gibbous moon
and she mourns
the things she can't hold.

# Acreage in the Highlands

If I hike for two hours, after riding a great blue heron and a snail, I can reach my grandfather's land: a mirage of pine knolls, banana trees, and creole palms. Across the *Camú* river in which my father bathed and my grandmother beat her clothes clean, beyond the creek where her cows drank the spring waters emanating from the haughty Central Range. Beyond Miranda mountain pregnant with gold. How many men claimed her, among myriad expecting hills snoozing unexplored? Beyond the tilted ground plowed by bulls and sown by hand before the sun coagulated on my uncles' shoulders and they couldn't carry the burden. Beyond the short barb wire fences delineating the rural pie. This, yours. This, mine. Generations of sun-beaten, horse-riding countrymen guarding each other's land long after entire families left the bighearted hills for the hapless valley, too far to see the stars parked over their forlorn huts when they looked up at night.

If I hike two hours to a place where cars cannot go and bicycles cannot reach, I can find my roots spread across the globe from Europe to Africa to the Middle East, to Asia. Only a part of me grows tuberous in the highlands where the Taino fled to escape the Spaniards.

That's the part of me that cries on the plane when I see my island; the part of me that craves cassava root and plantains, and the petrichor of native soil touched by the rain. That part of me understands why my father left this land, unspoiled and untapped, never to return.

*Insolence*

What nerve I have not to write
about broken bones and decaying flesh
lying faceless in the open,

or about the passersby flinching at their sight,
who will not stop because they are running
from their own blight.

Or about the abstaining rain
shunning our proud crops
because it wants kinder soils to fall on.

How we watch millennia burn in a purgatory
of sequoias and cheer crawls to higher ground,
away from us.

How dare I write

about the sun, and not about the monarchs
losing their homes, or about child sacrifice
by guns, or the drying wells and dwindling trust?

Why pick a petal from a living flower
as a token of joy, and not a tilling fork?

These days are dew and sweat
beading on my kitchen sponge
of a skin.

Thought forms dissolve like powder
in acid rain.

*Outrage makes house calls,*

and the goddess lost a finger
to all that reigns supreme.

These are brain fog and watermelon summers,
my love, but not the kind you can slice
with swords.

*Recycled Galaxies*

Madness is a burst of infinity
escaping through a rose window,

a blizzard of almond blossoms
befalling pastel blues,

an ascension of spent sunflowers
romancing cyclonic clouds.

It is recycled galaxies orbiting the same thought—
a cypress brushing against lost hope,

a gang of shadows sweeping the asylum
while stillborn angels keep the gate,

a sudden clearing
between two arches,

light reflecting on a pouring river
after a siesta on golden fields.

*Only for a Breath*

Silence shudders before the wind.
My pores stand in attention
to the waking beat.

I took pictures of a ram
settling disputes for the drove. He is still
a sheep.

But I am ether, grass and sea—
a fractal of a mountain
in the amalgamated ridge,

a complete tomorrow
when the moment still exists.
I am dispersed and collected,

in uncompromising dawns
that fade and last as long as I live.

I am free.

## Southern Home

# This home creeps around me

a mile a minute.
It covers my face until I morph
into the Earth Goddess (with an outstretched
hand, spewing water).

It bears roots before it chokes me
between the windows and misgivings.
I trip on the encroaching vines,
and touch can feel like cuffs
on breathless mornings.

It once smelled like joy, so I jellied
racemes of blossoms. I pickled the leaves,
made soup with the oblong roots
for as long as my hands could move.

Paralysis. I can't see the sun. The green
in my irises has dulled and winter is hopes away.
By then, I'll be gone. I'll be a wisp,
an apparition, a Southern ghost.

One day you will say

*I gave up on you,*

and you will be right.
I hid in the forest before you were born.
I learned its mysteries. I kept myself hidden
so that when we met, it would be pure joy.

I knew you would come
when my eyes started twinkling.
The *Tokoloshe*[1] circled me
but I could not see them.
There were no pebbles I could grab
from the lucid river.

They have crept into my heart while I slept.
Their whispers fill my head,
their cold hands grip my throat,
and their claws dig into my back
as they push and pull at memory, truth, and reality
until nothing makes sense anymore.

They are many, so they are strong,
but they are also weak because they are jealous
of what they can't conceive.
They can't create a better world
than the one they already see.

---

[1] *Tokoloshe*: In African folklore, a mischievous, mythical, manlike animal of short stature.

*Drifting Apart*

To endure your absence, I close
the windows, draw the velvet
curtains close to my chest.
That hefty fabric holds so much.

Until fall comes, and silence billows
like a wrinkled blanket over us.
The steaming iron's heat eases
our quibbles about the round Earth.

It keeps us warm
in our corners of the sea bed,
safe from the biblical rift, as we drift.

You won't know me anymore

if you leave me alone with winter,
and its retinue of frost.

*Broken Radar*

Every bloom is a feast to the hungry bees.
They don't mind that we haul them
to the almond fields.
Every flower gets a kiss.

Latitude is not freedom

without nectar.

Words revolt against a thought
unwinding from unknown spools,
the broken radar beats
a borrowed compass.

Who will survey the haunted forest
if not the lost,
the ones who can see the riddles
in the falling mist
and hear the clarion calls of wings
that will someday become extinct?

# There are poems for you

tucked under the old lamp
by my bedroom window.

They smell of swelled mahogany
and mosquito nets
grazed by the breeze.

They are written in print
so you can infer the tones in my ink,
and carefully etched from midrib to blade
in a banana leaf.

## That Time You Slipped

Let's talk about the things you cannot say,
how he left late in the spring, and

*you couldn't say goodbye;*

how unfair of the ether to let him gasp
for air as you held your breath,
hoping there would be time.

We prowl the dystopian field, barefoot
after the crash. Hot soil. Melted metal.
Notebooks halfway burnt. You pick one up
and go to school, as if your mind weren't
ground zero.

You learn about pennies, a religion
you'll never practice (the dry bones
of a world that doesn't know it died).

Stunted growth. I can eat on your head.
Your pocket full of dollars
tells me you're now a man. But a man wouldn't
slip on a river boulder and keep swimming,
without looking for their phone.

Submerged for five minutes and somehow
it still works. How hardy the superfluous,
and how fragile the requisite hands
you can no longer hold.

*Pinwheel*

The clarinet won't sing
without forced air,
and ivory missed the rainbow
of a pinwheel.

It's not your first choice,

but still...
It's less dire than to watch
you hyperventilate.

Electrodes can't surf
but they can tell
of the drowning of a heart
at a spiking wave.

I am saved
on the shoulders of a violin
moaning at a safe distance,
aching at the touch
of bow to string.

The flashing lights are retro-disco.
We can dance in the same room
as long as you blink,
and stay for the whole song,
and help me be strong
as you unlock the wind.

Not everyone who dances wants to be touched.
Her footprints dissipate like a thought
on the cozy tile.

The small town plaza has watched her grow.
Her sharp hips cleave the dense summer air,
her tropical flair, is an oleander bouquet.
Watch her dance but

*let her be.*

Not every flower you see wants to be picked.

# If love were a painting,

it wouldn't be the stark
blues and yellows of a Starry Night.
It would be an obscure cafe
in the South of France,
dotted with bistro tables cloaked in moonlight.
Patrons would eat and drink
with a blurred visage.
Pate and baguette, and a smudge of paint
in someone's half-bitten heart.

It would be a lonesome man
with trembling fingers, sowing the land.
His face, another blot
confronting the engorged sun,
befriending golden fields
so he can make a home.

Fighting for love is like fighting for air.

Love is an endowment we didn't ask for,
and need not share.
It is a gift from the solar beams
that gave us life.
We turn away from the ever sun,
and call it night.

Love is what's left

when we are stripped of stories.
It's what we are.

*Perspective*

Now that I have died,

and you've become a negative
running on a film
of a thousand lives,

I've forgiven your fingers,
(those sardonic imps)
for sins of omission.
I've ensconced your letters

in the epistolary
and bowdlerized our moments
of candor and desire.
I've rejoined the equanimous center

where columns tremble
and stillness speaks.
It told me we were lost in dioramas,
bemused by mirages

we had no need to dream.

Did you exert your hand
when you split the world right open
and it fell off your shoulders
so you could take a slice?

It was fresh like watermelon, thirsty as summer.
I tasted it when you kissed me, with a thrill
of recognition in your clear eyes.

It never had to be so hard.

Oh, how sadness is refined,

soft in places as it alights

like snow on placid mornings,
romantic as it lies

on spreads of its own blanket—
untarnished like old love,

buried under hot springs
welling with midnight thunder,

rumbling deep inside,
in no rush to serenade!

*Mending and Alterations*

You glimpse the outline
of my heart's recurring twilight.
You see me contemplating it,
and accompany me, in silence.

Then,

*why do you resign yourself*

to my half love, to my patches
stitched into a void
that only you could call a soul?

Why remain, to mend my brokenness,
and make me whole?

A summit of angels or an apex of shadows…
Inviolable beauty is inextricable from hell.

The blue-veined Earth stands out to heaven,
breastfeeding beings from glaciers to moraines:

the luminescent liars glinting in the dark, and

*the transparent truth,*

always seamless in daylight.

From ancient tree roots to the tallest mountain
peaks, she spreads her bounty equally
and graciously.

*Halfway to the Nuns' House*

I have held my breath for over forty years.
For the first twelve, my heart beat without sound.
On the walk to the nuns' house
from elementary school,
my backpack sags with fears and doubts.

A virgin awaits me halfway in the grotto,
shaded by ancient vines that shelter garden snakes.
She stamps one with one foot, the one
with eyes of Genesis, and Eden skin.

Oh, mother, do you see?
I'm only two pigtails away from my daydreams!
My bouncy spirit leaps at the midday sun.
I can't gaze directly at it.
When my backpack fills with fruit,
I will return to confront it with an exhale.

For now, the nun expects me to cross-stitch
my gifted project of a life into a larger fabric.
I sink and pull the needle
through the pre-made holes, stitching neatly
for extra effort

because there is no point.

# To exist in the white noise

between a breath and a thought,
modest and ignored, but soothing
like a calming wave that isn't strong
enough to move you,
but just warm enough
to keep you there…

Colors lean on April like a sentence
being carried up a slope.
She drags them slowly,
and vehemently.

There are purples

to atone for being numb.

There are reds
to beget after regret;

and there are yellows,
bright and mellow,
stroking every ache
to understand.

*If You Love Something*

I poach a bird with a word—
sharp-pointed and skin-dipped…
The mirage of a moment
fades to pixels on a black screen.

Tomorrow gathers its feathers
and pops them on,
ready to fly away from my hands.

I let it go, for it is mine.

Is it true that all rivers rush to the sea?

I've seen at least one scurrying upstream,
fleeing the enormity of one.

That dreaded unity,

frothing into foam at the height of flow,
gazes lower at the end of a wave,
capitulating, outworn and nameless,
to the shore.

Your shadow follows you.
I let mine lead.

We have deserts to sow, and

*my shadow knows*

where the ground is soft enough to give,
before the rain muddles my feet.

The sun hops on my back.
My basket is full of knicks and knacks.

I carry it, not for the stuff,
but for the weavers.

*All I Need*

To be in my body of soaring swallows,
inhaling enough jasmine for flight,
open-beaked after dusk
precipitates into the night...

To be a paradox of blue
with bands of umber over tame white,
to ingest

futility as vital nourishment,

and always nest in your rustic barn...

## The Long Way Home

We take the long way home, after
denying ourselves a grave. I don't want to stain
the windows and watch you go
through the colored glass.
I slip into clouds, and mind my every step,
waist-deep in manners, so as to not
wake the dead.

I walk through a graveyard of past lives.
My feet sink and squelch in the muck
of long-forgotten objects that no longer feel
like mine.
The ground is littered with broken things—
moments that were once whole, now shattered
into pieces: a discarded watch here, a yoga mat
there… rusty keys from old tenants
who left their luggage intact.

The sky has swelled so much
since I emerged from her bosom,
but when I glance outside,

I still feel like a bubble

floating within her breasts.
Someday, I will burst, sun-pricked,
and someone will finally see me:
with my eyes closed and lips smiling peacefully,
as if dreaming of something wonderful.

Along the edge of clouds
our eyes unlearn the sky
diffusing white and gray
over the stark horizon.

Where can we go

that our instincts haven't been?
What animal can we draw
between euphoria and rain?

I will sketch a soaring condor,
and meet you eagerly
at the edge.

I prune myself for air,
so that my flowers can attract the bees.

*But only you can see me*

through the green and the overgrowth,

beyond the untapped humus,
and the fine compendiums
of my grandfather's land.

It sits among hills and marrow,
waiting for us to bear fruit.

*Plum Blossoms*

Here you are,
slurping winter's last straw,
*blooming despite yourself*
on a random sidewalk.

Why wield your pink sword
to slice the air in half?
Part of it slaps my face
for every unspoken insolence,

for my silent revolt
against too many consonants.
Some of it lurks beneath my feet
embracing my roots with an incongruous chill.

Once this is over, I won't look at you twice.
You'll be just one more green compromise
on my way to the next blossom.
And I will be just another figure in black,

a silhouette without a name
you will recognize through the rustling leaves.

# Part II: Dust and Pine

So that you'll hear me
my words sometimes grow thin
as the tracks of the gulls on the beaches.
Necklace, drunken bell
for your hands as smooth as grapes.
And I watch my words from a long way off.
They are more yours than mine.
They climb on my old suffering ivy.

~ Pablo Neruda

# Half of you left with her,

or maybe after her, two steps behind
her bright, red aura.

Part of you grifts with the monarchs
from milkweed to zinnia to
a balcony of pretense.

The rest of you is here, earthbound
shade, crisp morning air infusing
the apple in my hand.

She wore feathers in her hair,
poppies on her chest, and sap
on her skin.

She was frail and thin
in places where hope fades
with the sun's flare.

She once inflamed the buoyant sky
to tint the air.

Now she lights candles for the lonely moon
to see its glare.

She decks her hut with golden wreaths,

*in case he cares.*

I knew it was time
to uncork the night upon your chest,
knee-deep in the morass
of incandescence,

*to disrobe your essence*

of its sweet arrogance
encrusted like mica
under my skin—

to sup your refined grin,
conjuring rainbows,
and adagios that tremble
deeply within.

The brooding sun pops over lopsided hills.

*What obsession!*

What madness to turn up every day in pursuit
of a flower who once said it needed light.

Or was it a blade of grass subdued by dew,
desperate for heat to feel free?

Or was it a poet
who misplaced their moon?

You became my poetry,
impalpable wool skin
in the wintering.

Hapless are we, who found
the place that plunges warmly
within but didn't leap.

Afflicted, my sallow hands seek you

*in the asininity of words*

that never quite arrive.

*Dust and Pine*

No more will you find me
staring out the window at logs
split by chance,
disparaging their sapience.

You will not see me crestfallen,
baptized by the rain
on the heretic fall of the path,
wearing white.

As I look to the east,

*I will no longer long*

for dust and pine.

Allegory of a dream…
Pupils burn in the doughy
ethereal field.

From shadow and ground, light and sound,
strands spin into cocoons
of clarity and desire.

This is where we meet,

where delirium grows like branches
in the subtlety of the night.

You,
a quiver of dawn in the valley,
the canyons of a twilight sigh.
Days awaken and sleep with you,
engulfed in your ardent hues.

Ochre reigns when the horizon cedes,
a subtle show of fondness, or a promise
to falter before settling again

*in your afterglow.*

In the end, fire dies.

It exhausts into form
from the supernal, fueling
a constellation of ash
we dispel with Jack-Pine hands.

*We don't burn. We seethe*

in the ambit of a breath
laid on embers beyond
our reach.

He slips—
like dew on morning leaves
evaporates within me.

# I ran through the white noise

toward the melodic humming.

I swept aside fractured memories
into empty graves, like spicules
sucked into a curly void.

I don't know how deep it goes
but I still run toward the melody,
to the dawning of your silken voice
over my skin.

There is space for a forest behind this heart.
Live oak and Spanish moss would thrive.

There's always room for pine

between the metered verses and the futile lines.

I would love some redwoods and sequoias
to uplift the land but the tears won't dry.

Don't ask me why.

Is it fog, or is it smoke?

There is nothing left

but a hollow of sequoias
where the gales turned.
It once was our abode
before Earth began to run.

Everyone has a tree where they thought
they would build a home.
Ours is a pit of charred mementos
where the two of us burned.

Night descends over rolling hills,
impious, resigned to be a prelude
to the day's fugue.

Moonlight sifts through

*your diaphanous skin,*

as it shimmers onyx and gold.

Emerald rivers rush below, an avalanche
of softness, the broken waves
of a love song, refracting.

Why does water ride the corruptible wind?

She is giddy on his shoulders,
as heavy as yesterday.
He spins her into vortexes and storms.
They find a house to turn to stardust
from sticks and stones.

She is reduced
to a molecule of dew.

*So she grows and waits*

to begin anew.

The rainbow never showed after all this rain.
Now the sun won't thaw these frigid hills.

Truth lives in the silence,

and dies with it, pristine and tranquil,
and unfulfilled.

*Past Midnight*

He was there, in my forever dome,
among casual memories,
resting on my bed of amber and dust.

I moaned hello, asked how he was
with an almost pang of lust,
excitement creeping beneath my clothes.

I steeped in his rum halo
to soothe my triggered pores,
and woke up at four.

There is freedom, perhaps, in ignoring our ties,
spinning to the right or deciding what's left to try.

Irrespective of our plan, we are paced
by the shrewdest hands while we wade
this lazy river,

*clueless that we orbit love,*

for better or worse, as if by hypnosis.

*The Small Print*

As long as you know
that my hips won't fill your hands
with apples and plums,
you're welcome to touch.

It is not that the wind eroded my flesh
as I slept lifetimes on ivory beds.
Nor did I bleed torrents
of virgin skies on my way to Venus.

As long as you know
that my brew won't fill your cup
no matter how much I pour,
you're welcome to drink.

I won't quench your thirst.

I am more jasmine and patchouli,
less wine and bread.

*The Price of Silence*

Those who leave with words unsaid,
pluck them from the ether
and tuck them in their chest.
They nurture them like chick ravens
chirping in the nest.

Claustrophobic and ravenous,
they peck and peck,
sipping thick blood
until they're old enough
to fly on their own.

Then, they burst the heart.

When I stared at the sky of your hallowed
silhouette, and you stared back,

*stars swallowed me whole*

in stark infatuation.

I descended to the place where worlds beg
to be born to atone for silence.
But there is nothing I can say
you don't already know,
since you were just as low.

# If I forget you

in the convulsion of a lunar day,
when earthshine is pointless
to those who don't seek light,
and my heart won't leap
when your name drowns the night.

If aortic emblems don't bear your mark,
and your shadow won't inflect my harmonies,
allow me the respite.

I am not sure which came first,
the almost-spark or the stirred wind—
pyromaniacs in love,

*ablaze with the first touch.*

The ubiquitous smoke
leering our instincts…

Our bodies in immolation,
an afflicting pseudo art
of scorched daisies,
and fresh starts.

To the girl who left those poems
spent and withered by the riverbank,
and ran away before I could say hi:

I read every word.

I dreamt and cried.
I plucked twelve petals from a field of daisies,
and made you a cot where your soft can lie.
It's by the fireflies.

*Neither Here Nor There*

Twilight has a name I can't pronounce,
so I hide when she comes out
looking for me.

The north is cold and prim,
primed for a painting
of a snow-capped, jagged dream.

But you, ruby-throated hummer
like to glide south to my wintering grounds
to feed while I sleep.

Poetry, and other ways to sublimate life,
so a loveless day may feel less harsh...

Her hands on a piano, the inexorable sighs, and
rain on verdant fields turned brown,
rain flooding doorways and emptying eyes,

rain deserting my impervious body
*lush with longing*—

tonight.

Pay no mind to the love-blemished stars
tainting the firmament with scintillated lies,
awash with anguish at sharing the spotlight
with the ever moon.

Once a feeble maiden awaiting the sun
to beam her into life,

she is now a beacon

for lonely poets adrift at night.

I am not here
sucking nectar for lack of fruit,
crushing verbena in your hands
so you can numb my pain,

or knead me with faint I love yous
as quasi-palliatives

for the rift inside my chest,

for the chasm that ends all hollows,
where a river sings me awake
every time I drift.

And love dictates we write
with loath plumes and feathers aimed at the sky,
erasing tattered clouds shrouding the desert sun,
filling the lacunas where only words flow.

It demands we journey to where we belong—
that we say I'm sorry, I've missed you,

I was wrong.

He didn't want my hands sowing his field.
I didn't need his eyes surveying my worth.

There were

landforms between us.

The sun was blinding above.

A sullen skyline I couldn't dream of
hugged the desert below.

The rubble rising was not a phoenix,
and love was not the backdrop.

I hold you loosely in my hands,
as if gravity were nonexistent.

Some days you're so small
you could ride on my breath,
and I wouldn't know that

I live for you.

Sometimes I am lost
until you rain on me,
and find me picking mushrooms
off my skin.

# Words are pointless

when each mind is a universe,
and stars are still forming
behind your stoic eyes.

It is too late for daffodils
but Spring still snoozes
one more dream of love.

Will you absolve the heavens
if my hands burst with tulips
to adorn your Venus
prancing above?

You mold my face with empty hands,
and cast distant autumns into dark
circles under my eyes.

You touch me with weary fingers
where time wields its hold
upon the hive.

You stay the rain, honey and stone
upon my meadows,

*and still I melt*

like a sun-wrecked honeycomb.

*Landscape Painting*

I was once a long-lobed leaf
soaking eternity amid pastel blues,
toasty and golden as I faced the sun
cresting your canvas.

I was a jut of bliss
protruding the horizon
with my pinnate lines.

And your brush felt fine,
polite and gentle as

*you diffused my veins.*

*The Naked Woman in the Painting*

# She seems different

when I look at her, sitting in this old chair.
Her body is more like a pear
than a sphere of woe.

She won't look at me sideways,
her eyes fledged with sadness
if I dare speak your name.

I can suddenly exhale,
when her pathos veers
into the oblique trains of yore.

*Snapdragon Bed*

Oh, how you keep me
heart-bound in color-filled towers,
guarded by dragons
in canary and pink!

They scorched my violets
when they snapped,
roared and breathed fire
on this naked spring.

I still smile for you,

a plain desire
that wanes with the hours
to be stoked anew.

# There was no message

under the leaves,
only a crushing sound
turned into mush…

footprints too faint
to break the skin,
scarlet nothings,
boudoir release.

How long have you loved me?
The mist pools in my wings
as I jump from leaf to leaf.
Dew is heavy in this heat.
You're no charming prince

but there is luster in the air, and

*in love, all is fair*

as my mage dispels the shadows,
and flies with midday swallows
to turn a new leaf.

This is where I come
to commune with diamonds,
and retrieve the gems you left
in my ears,

sweet nothings that sparkle
every time I retract, and

*you explode with light*

from each dimension of breath,
leaving specks of moonstone
in the dwindling falls.

# He is never coming back,

not like he was when we first met
Hallelujah, and his hair was as stubborn
as it was indulgent between my fingers,
and his body was a shrine where I paid
my penance, and I could see my reflection
in his lofty silence after every orison
was heard.

*Monotony*

We knew to stay the course,
heartened by morning and birdsong,
turning the hourglass
every time the sand ran low.

We made the bed and warmed the stove.
We cooked the meals and ate the words,

*awaiting a spark of magic,*

and a thrill with no parallel.

Through my moon-charged heart,
and my sunflower pores,
I can feel your sparkle
with my eyes closed.

You stole those clear diamonds
from a collarbone of night
to be the bustier
of a topless sky.

And how you shine,

*pixelated under my eyelids*

with your scarlet shadow,
and iridescent mind.

The frown that elucidates
the closed dawn of your palm
before a silent sea,
has filled with yesterdays
romping in its wounded bull trenches.

And

*you bleed, open chested*

in fluvial anguish of molten suns,
while my little boat dodges
desperate flickers of failed dusks.

# I get tired of diving

in your unfathomable pauses,
where years are silent ripples,
and when they rest, you fade…

into drops of a placid never
that lulls in the seamless blue
beneath my pores.

I wish we had been softer
than our instincts while riding
the whale's back.

Had I tied you to my wavelength,
you wouldn't have crashed on clouds
when it jumped out of the water
to catch a breath.

We wouldn't have sunk like a leaden cloak,
had you tempered my fears
on the deep dive home.

But you didn't.
But I didn't.

That's why static won the race
between the wings and the waves,
why we can't glide or swim in

what we left behind.

First, you die a scorching dream,
and I bury you under the moon garden,
with stars on each shoulder to gather the dust.

I cry crushed blueberries.
Tell you with stains
what the day never could.

How the game starts when you trip
on one domino, and topple my life
*without making a move.*

The rain never stopped falling,

even after the sky quit,
the clouds left,
and the Earth succumbed
to eclipsed silhouettes.

It poured on the orphan fields
of the ruddy desert,
on the digression of a mountain crest,
on the absurdity of

a day without you.

You well in my eyes
like a private memory,
a happy story that was once true,

*before our timeline vanished*

behind the sundial.

We still chase its shadow
for a moment of ecstasy
that never moved.

*In the acoustics of summer,*

finches and hummingbirds chirp
millennial love songs in my ears.

I hear them flow.
Only now can water glow,
eternal as a sunray over the velvet curtains
of my eyelids.

And a book can read me
as easily as your fingers
but prefers to sing me instead.

I scry the eddy
for a glimpse of you,
and other things I lost
in the swirls of chance.

You are still there

with your eyes on the hill
packed with mockingbirds
that steal your voice.

They profess your love with
their dusk-drunk notes.
Please rest and wake me
with sober tones of dawn.

# I'm stuck in the warrens

of an unknown place
learned by rote during endless nights
where your voice enfolds the dark
like a second skin.

Quicksilver jolts,
rivers of gold and onyx
reach an eldritch pitch.
And the wind sits so still,
giving no hint of an address.

Wild poppies burn
in your idea of heaven.
As long as you are alive,
I hold the earth in my hands.

I can no longer see you

through molten asphalt and pine.
It is my own myopia
or a blessing in disguise.

White horses roam in my idea of heaven,
and poppies bloom alongside.

# You, the unsolvable allegory

sauntering stealthily from dusk to dusk.
I strain my eyes to trace your silhouette
against the chiseled, roaring night.

The Leo sun devours you
just to show you off
but all I see is blood pooling at my feet
from desiccated roses.

Linger a little longer.

*This is a dream for two.*

Your fingers doodle in the wine. An eddy flows
through my belly, chasing away
the seagulls.

An impending breath tenses the air.
Where did the sun go?
It's just a bistro table on the beach,
and the two of us.

# I want my old lovers

partying together at Elbow Room.
I won't be there.
They all know each other anyway.
They are bound by the same, fragile tie—
but it's not me.
It's their hidden tenderness only I could see,
their daredevil child tearing through life,
waving at me.

My feet have hardened in warm, dense clay.
My adobe bark is your abode
now that it keeps you from the ominous rain.
These days,

*your throat is dammed*

with rigid boulders where words once flowed.
Yet I sense an intimation of love
reverberating in the hollow.

*Craving Nectar*

It's been years since I held a brush but
I can't stop painting your face,
paper aster with purple petals,
and a fragrant, yellow heart.

Butterflies flock to this garden

*uncertain as to why*

but bees know your taste,
crisp apple on a curious tongue
that has never known solitude.

I grow from you,
long-legged and thin-skinned.
My limbs are willows, unhollowed
veins of you.

Beneath the earth, the underworld
weaves my roots into your feet.

You grow the joyous greenery
of a budding day,
and summer's transient beanstalks
clawing at a fading dream.

Sometimes
*love is a command,*

and not a feeling—
a gut-waking flutter
with one's marching orders.

Conviction stark as a comet,
long-tailed and infrequent...

The dust tail lingers
long enough to veil the sun.

It's a topic of conversation
among astronomy enthusiasts,
and my pen.

# He has nothing new to say.

This cheerless summer is packing up,
eager for the train home
(a forever winter, perhaps,
where it can make its mark).

He is so still. I'm afraid

he has jelled into my skin.
I am not savvy about men,
I am not sure how to love them
once the nights get colder.

Ascending notes, exalted breath...
Nights on a balcony suffused the sluggish twilight.

I emerge from you,

my catharsis, on a turquoise beach.

You are lifeless in this *hiraeth*[2].
So, I carry you like a hero in my rucksack,
torpid in my blood, weightless in the sea.

---

[2] Hiraeth: (Welsh word) Longing for a home you cannot
return to, or that never existed.

Late summer Monardas replenished
these wildflower meadows.

I see you from afar, the ruse
of distance rekindling our flame.

Your dilly of a smile
fills my fissures with red jasper.

I've grown old watching you

sort this wild meadow,
this scarlet garden.

I'd forgotten how different we are.
Your shadow falters between dregs
of fondness and mildewed memories
of a steam shower out west.

Two flinty minds atilt,

*risking a nexus...*

You, dammed to the ends
of your thick brown hair.
I, bleeding out over it
without making a dent.

I have no claim to your makeshift home,
even though you intended to build
a castle where I would turn to stone.

*It is better this way.*

I clamber into my hut between scraggly trees,
won't carp about the aches in my back.
Fireflies kiss my eyelids, and I dream
of yellow roses.

I sit, rigid and still,
as you present your gift.
It's wrapped in mystery,
or maybe it's a ruse
to get me out of this rut.

Your promise is like a rose
making its entrance,
as a hand of ribbons unwraps
to reveal its song.

And yet,

*I can't hear you*

through the thorns.

*So You Think*

Because you see me, and I
didn't call you, you emanate
from the lake, my only mirror.

In your sword point, the water ripples
with irreplicable waves.

My hands are weak—
unable to trace my lips with liner
to fill a day.

So you, my savior, defy stillness

to fill your void.

How loosely do we hold the ambiguity
of a whim before it slips
to bathe a rose?

He still lives somewhere,

in the liquid entrails
of a dream.

His hair is wet and thick.
I drift in the abysm
of his chest and lose my grip

until I emerge,
muddied and cold
in a bed of rain.

*Pool of Ink*

It's four am at the peeking twilight
of my youth.
A lullaby is pinned to my head
with a thumbtack.

You, holding our crying baby,
your neck wrung just so
you could beam your vehemence
at me.

A tenderness I seldom touched,
and no one deserves.
Tears baptizing my cheeks,
consecrating them.

And this pen. This pen,
reminding me of
all the moments left unlived.

*"Men are from Mars, Women…"*

We reclaim our bodies
after the ecstasy,
parsing dusk like judges
in the shivering night.

You school lake fish
in useless manners,
how to engage a lady
who is more of a vice.

How Mars always acts

while Venus retracts,
versed in the vulnerable
vainglory of men.

He picks me from a see-through garden
of lilies and marigolds in cellophane.
Time rolls its eyes,
hemmed in and carved into tree bark.

Whispers fill the hollow in his back, sutured
by a straight jacket from a Seraphim
only he can see. He also sees me, since

*he's colorblind.*

Shatterproof bottles form a gallery
of long-neck memories filled with wine.

*October in Napa,*

an Indian summer of slow-footed zinfandels...

Your French nose diving into the night's throat,
a guitar ennobling the acoustic mind–
the indolent anguish of our thighs…

Indisposed and cranky but still here.
Do I get attendance points?

Days moo me awake, unfurling
like fronds in this farmed jungle.

I lay my amphora of molten gripes
with the rest of the tribe. Privileged,

I waltz to the fair breeze and resent it for the
dance

*because I miss you.*

You who cross the indomitable highlands
of my sorrows to drink the toxic sap of my skin,
have my regard.
They dispel your phantom touch
against a frazzled sky.

Mornings aren't mornings

in these shrouded woods.
Hooded cloaks kidnap the dawn
among your tattered whispers.

You exhume my body
after I died in your arms
a half-life ago.

Earthworms, noble alchemists,
gutted the lacunas
of my lovesick bones.

Look closely. I don't exist.

Your hands will not stick
to my gossamer skin,
despite how much you feel my everything.

If I were looking for answers,
I would find them floating
in the flirtation of a gold-mistified,
clear day.

Oceans would part so I could see

your chipped-stone of a heart

exiled from the feeling earth.

It would be a mirage,
a sight for feeble minds:
obsidian drowning in blue,
and thanking it.

# There's nothing back there.

I've already looked.
My eyes capered in the entrails
of the black hole that is you.
My feet have learned to read the tides,
to befriend and feed the duplicitous sand.
I hold washed sunsets in my hands
to fill the empty sockets
of my moonless face.

I ride the rump of this torpid morning.
Its hind legs dredge molasses
between my woolen lips.

What to say to the disgruntled arbiter
of our sins, committed despite the moonlight
slapping our hips awake
so we couldn't miss its touch?

I'm sorry love.
I'm always sorry.

# Part III: The Last Trace of Us

the circle goes round
without any bridges
the river comes through
with goldfish in it
our hearts jump in
we holding hands
as we float along
to other lands

~ Nikki Giovanni

Bit by bit, my eyes were blurred
until things became smudges,
and people, stains.
Cities lost their skyline,
countries, their name.
My legs became skeins
of ashy thread.
My navel vanished.
My spine fell next.
My chest imploded.
My lips evanesced.

I am but a smear

of a former self.

It just wasn't enough
that we christened the sun,
and groomed it for the day
with cedarwood and musk,

that sirens sang its praises
from cardamon to dusk—

that our crowns lengthened
in pious salutations
for its hard-earned nod.

*It was all in vain.*

We never felt its warmth,
and it never saw our face.

Before it all ended,

*we saved what we could*:

a scoop of earth,
a torn envelope filled with seeds,
the smile of a child
whose face just felt the rain,
the frisson of a first touch—
hubris,
the smell of promise on
youthful skin…
cherry blossoms,
a floating maple leaf
in a jar of crisp November.

Our prayers eroded from the mound
of complaints and supplications.

We, children of the night,
uneasy at every dusk, disturbed
by gaunt reflections of our lack
of trust.

Our sunken faces had room
for hope.
Desire left us long ago, bereft and tailing

*the last trace of us.*

## Primal Robe

It is a constant fear of mine,

or perhaps a premonition
that we'll be stripped of our garments
down to the primal robe.
We will strike rocks again to start a fire,
and gather around it at night
to reminisce about the days
when we could tweet and chat.

Far above us, the stars
will again be daunting strangers;
the moon, a brooding goddess or a smirking hag.
We will no longer see the chords tying the sea
to her moving hands, but she will remember
who we were before she unleashed the tide.

We will hunt and gather, explore and forage,
and kneel to the god of rain
as he watches in disdain,
with his pipe in one hand.
We will ride cracked, vinyl boats,
and test our grit through a deluge of spite.
There is only one saving grace: duck tape
still exists in this other life.

My family passes by,
and invites me to come aboard.
I step off the slippery boulder
into the things I know.

It can happen at any time,
the road fades into my shadow
and I can no longer drive.

*I find my honesty,*

and accept I'm blind.

That's when innocence pulls
up in her chariot and offers me a ride.
Only she knows the destination
but the wonder is all mine.

Green dots punctuate the hazed horizon.

*We pray to fertility gods*

for a semblance of rain
to grace our arid fields
with mana and hope.

The kind that grows inside,
shrewd as a seed,
who knows how much to grow,
and what to be.

I was just contemplating the world,
how superlatives claim
the dystopian streets abandoned
for cozy, unlit corridors.

How I'm a thread
in your epic web
feeling the vibes
of helpless prey.

They seem to dance

*on a spiral of doom,*

swaying their way
toward a manic end.

*Redress*

This fogged mirror has room
for one more ghost. I carry a few
on my back and can't feel them
when I duck to splash my face.

Tap water runs the length of a thought,
or a string of them, pinned to rotting wood—
pretending ambiance is a redress
to decay.

No one asks how I define
the spirit world. It's like looking for lost lore
among the living. The dead keep pinning
their half-colored pages to our clean mirrors.

Sometimes we see them

and use our own markers to fill the empty
space, for show and tell.

During camp nights, we share
our redeemed stories, while leaning
against decaying wood that somehow
still stands.

*War*

# Who will hold the children

when the ground crumbles under their feet,
and their hands have but one prayer
left to resist?

Who will open their umbrella
to muffle the sky
when hell has no lollipops,
and the subway, no sunshine?

*Bowl of Stew*

She'll wear a crown of Larimar
when fragments of exploded
satellites tear her roof.

She knows it's time to run

somewhere, but the basement
is full of dragons, and other giant, mystic
creatures waiting for a saving ark.

The attic is scooped open,
a bowl of fear and children
huddled in a corner, looking up.

But he… he's in the kitchen, eating
a stew with five meats and roots.
He's been through this before,
an alien invasion, the end
of an age, a recession.

He's seen Gaia change her dress
from a leaf, to cotton, to silk.
Soon, she'll don her steel gown
and walk in the sun with arms
wide open, to melt in its grace.

*Zooming In on the Bowl of Stew*

Huddled under the roof of a thunderous morning,
our hands became bowls, our heads,
cascade fountains.

*Our bodies filled like vases*

of thirsty dahlias. We suffered the fever
of a blunt shear's cut, and sought each other's feet,
to find only immanence.

In this desecrated cave, echoes
fly like shards and splinter our ears.

We bleed nostalgia

and siren song over the unrisen buck moon.

Our souls flood in perigee, our bodies
scatter into myriad yens over cosmic seas.

I sense your eyes in every quasar
girded in waves of blue.

Neptunian veils protect us—
a polyandry of intangibles with solid rock…
Flitting butterflies intoxicate the moment,
while the earth unfolds readily under our feet.

We can't seem to breathe,
so we withhold, and

measure the empty space

from our charged solar plexus
to the other end of the energetic chord.

*Shadow Work*

Self-destruction is an art,
a right of passage in the cosmic play.
Little voices spread from their origami fold—
a slow reveal of shades and shadows.

I saw and fell

*this paper forest of figures*

that won't hold their shape in the rain,
or let the sunbeams in.

# Demons don't roam the dark,

little lamb.
They are radiant and soft-spoken.
Their hands will trace your needs
until they harden beneath your eyelids
like unstated grace:
unattainable, unforgettable.

*Pity this bleary pen.*

It doesn't know
when or how the story ends,

or who will knit a fitting shroud
for its ceasing pulse.

It awaits a solar flare, an augury
of blue jays at the feeder
in warmer months,

or a dimensional tear
where your words mark a period
of gain and loss.

# I channel these words

that aren't mine
because they circle innocuous souls,
ones who can't see the sharks in the water
until they spill blood.

You never knew me to think
beyond the carvings of salvaged wood
shaped by sweat and calloused hands
but refined to the touch.

More than anything,

*I wanted air.*

I died every two seconds
from that vitiated breath.

I learned to spruce my flaws
to annoy the unnatural.

My back blocked the stones
as I tumbled downhill in the fetal position.

I am now stalled, bruised, and clothed
by my understory.

The sun is home, petting his cat
while the moon pours her bowl
on the frazzled world.

She conceals her breasts with one hand.

She is always naked.

Why hide when we don't look up?

Today, stars align swiftly on her collarbone.
She lathers her onyx locks
with glowworm bars.

*Prepping for a Lonely Day*

Fall is not yet here but I am
hoarding wheat.
There is plenty of room for things
since I let go of stories.

Seasons fit neatly inside my cargo joggers.

Spring was not meant to be
the sole augur of new beginnings,
so I pocket it with fall,
and a sylph of crisp air for company.

In this marble tower,
ribbons and tendrils leaven me
until I rise.

The world parades below me
as I stare out the window.
People are fireflies.

Time has left me savvy and nimble
but it is no longer my North Node.

I wonder if you see me

from your marble tower,
and what color ribbons you sew.

Isn't sacredness the mimicry
of that which brings us awe?

I tiptoe around a leaf. It falls as it yips.
I French-manicure my nails
to trace your lips with a *je ne sais quoi*.

We return to silence, this bliss
between our bubbles.
The candle flickers and

I, too, hesitate.

This garden bed is a chest of instants.
Boulders fret between coneflowers,
idle but alive.

Hummingbird loops are fleeting like youth.
Her salty wet hair grumbles with tangles.

A reluctance of needles pine for summer light,
jealous of leaves that turn colors

before giving up the fight.

*Even now, I shrug*
at the night's reproachful silence.
How did I pierce its ego in the acicular
bargain of a day?

I rewrote my cheerless lines
under the umbra of an old live oak.

Birds chirp above my own
chatter, spiteful of the looming
darkness, in tacit solidarity.

They only come out at night—
mauve lips and faux, gold lashes

*poking at the demure moon.*

She, too, knows how to play
when the world has drawn its curtains
but still lifts its brows
peeking behind the velvet
and sipping rum.

Kisses (never French),
keep the seas at bay…

I undress the rose, despite the platitude,
crushing petals on my tongue to dull my voice.
Playing with the banal means
stepping on the naked stem.

*Pain as an initiation*

for misconceived humanity,
bloody punctures in the fascia
of a crusty heel… as a wink to love.

There are corners in my room
eons away from innocence.
My child cowers behind the flames,
aflutter with incandescence,

*phobic of the world*

raging outside the window.

I'm so glad, she says, we're not from here.
I cool her with my tears, promise
to take her home.

A geisha adorns the misty path
with rice powder face, and sealed lips.
She performs a demure dance,
revered art of rigid hips,
and a tea ceremony, where she can utter
inaudible whispers to a Bloodgood maple.
She is a shell. Bound body
and motes for feet, because

*nobody traps a soul.*

*Identity Crisis*

Every fall feels the same,
staring out at a maybe sea
from the promontory.

Fingers chafe in an edgy interlace.

A narrowing trail seems to push it
into the ambivalent sea.
Another year, another quandary:

*to be or not to be*

a soft-landing cloud, a crash site,
or a trampoline to winter,
cold and slick.

Old bones hold memory, and
*everything I released*
because it weighed down my arms.

Now I spin wildly and freely
under those ancient palms,

collapsing in bliss
on carpets of sand

with your warmth on my skin
and your hand on my hand.

*Monarch*

She stretches one leg as I approach,
and sips from a yellow straw.
A play of light blurs every leaf
beyond her fanning organza wings.

She doesn't mind me,

or care that I am big.
She knows she is as lithe as the breeze
and can fly away much faster
than I could reach.

## Zinnia Garden

Whose shade do you seek
on these sun-chided days?
Whose weeping willow veils you in sorrow
as it shields you from the rain?

Whose garden fascinates you
with its vibrant landscape?
Words can fog the air with grumble and dust.
Only my zinnias give me food for thought.

*May Pansies*

She still breathes, thyme-scratched by mid spring
among a million faces that cower from heat.

*She believes—*

an anxiety of pansies singing to the sun…
as they wilt.

I came from the earth,
and yet I have never returned.

I left my roots in the compact
grievances of a forest.
I shed my bark on the sixth day,
grew a heart, and two legs.

Now I roam unbound,
zapped by electric clouds

*whenever I stray*

too far from the ground.

He holds me in his breath,
propped by gravity on organza leaves.

There are forests of jade
sighing between our lips.

I never want to leave.

Let me swing from limb to limb
in the zest of this moment.

Stretch languidly
in the morning's midrib
until you're bathed
by a tumble of dew.

Savor the honeycomb
where the days halt in honey
and utopia sets in
when your smile is in view.

Stroll with me

*into the heart of summer*

before the year sheds its shell
to grow it anew.

I traced the rough edges of infinity after
time finally died.

It flickered in my field of vision
like a wavering mirage—
so alien... sublime!

I welded myself to a moment,
and it felt grand
to ride on its contrails,
and feel the heft of its presence
in mine.

If this day should never end,

*I will decipher the meaning*

in a bout of refrain,

I'll untangle the roots
in a network of pain.

I will watch emancipated
songbirds after the rain,

and a cloud cabaret
taunting the earth.

I would pray we learn from iteration
to be more humane.

# Thank you for reading!

If you enjoyed this poetry collection,
please leave a review and
tell me what resonated with you.

## MORE POETRY BY ANTONIA WANG:

*Love Bites: Poetry & Prose*

*In the Posh Cocoon: Poetry and Bits of Life*

*Hindsight 2020: Brief Reflections on a Long Year*

*Retrospectiva 2020: Reflexiones Breves Sobre un Año Largo*

*Palette: Love Poems and Painted Words*

# Acknowledgments

Versions of these poems have appeared or are forthcoming in the following publications:

- "Acreage in the Highlands" - page 19 - *Heron Clan X* (Poetry Anthology)
- "Only for a Breath"- page 24 - *Setu Magazine*
- "Southern Home"- page 25 - *Setu Magazine*
- "Broken Radar"- page 28 - *Setu Magazine*
- "Pinwheel" - page 31- *SpillWords Press*
- "Halfway to the Nuns' House" - page 40 - *Hidden in Childhood* (A Poetry Anthology)
- *"Primal Robe" - page 135 - Heron Clan X* (Poetry Anthology)
- "Redress"- page 139 - *SpillWords Press*


Many thanks to Ty Gardner, an outstanding poet whose work I follow and admire, for lending his keen eye to the editing of this collection.

My appreciation to the #vss365 and #FromOneLine writing prompt organizers on Twitter, who inspired early versions of many of these poems with their literary prompts.

To my readers: thank you!

# About the Author

Antonia Wang is the Amazon best-selling author of Love Bites, In the Posh Cocoon, Hindsight 2020, Retrospectiva 2020, and Palette. She is an international CASS scholar originally from the

 Dominican Republic. Her work has been praised for its vibrant imagery and thoughtful exploration of themes such as love, loss, and identity. Her distinctive lyrical style has been featured in several literary journals and anthologies. She writes in English and Spanish.

Antonia draws inspiration from her world travels, Caribbean heritage, and 18-year yoga practice. She lives with her family in the United States.

Website: biteslove.com
Twitter & Instagram: @tuttysan